KAMALA HARRIS

First Female US Vice President

BY LAURA K. MURRAY

CONTENT CONSULTANT
RACHEL BLUM, PhD
DEPARTMENT OF POLITICAL SCIENCE
UNIVERSITY OF OKLAHOMA

An Imprint of Abdo Publishing | abdobooks.com

abdobooks.com

Published by Abdo Publishing, a division of ABDO, PO Box 398166, Minneapolis, Minnesota 55439. Copyright © 2022 by Abdo Consulting Group, Inc. International copyrights reserved in all countries. No part of this book may be reproduced in any form without written permission from the publisher. Essential Library™ is a trademark and logo of Abdo Publishing.

Printed in the United States of America, North Mankato, Minnesota.
052021
092021

Cover Photo: Sait Serkan Gurbuz/AP Images
Interior Photos: Andrew Harnik/AP Images, 4; Marcio Jose Sanchez/AP Images, 9; AP Images, 14, 19; Richard Cummins/Alamy, 24; Mary F. Calvert/MediaNews Group/The Mercury News/Getty Images, 29; Eric Slomanson/Zuma Wire/Alamy, 32; George Nikitin/AP Images, 35; Jeff Chiu/AP Images, 37; Rich Pedroncelli/AP Images, 42, 54; Damian Dovarganes/AP Images, 46, 49; Paul Sakuma/AP Images, 51; Jose Luis Magana/AP Images, 58; Tony Avelar/AP Images, 64; Wilfredo Lee/AP Images, 68; Michael Brochstein/Sipa USA/AP Images, 72; Bill Clark/CQ Roll Call/AP Images, 74; Susan Walsh/AP Images, 78; Carolyn Kaster/AP Images, 81, 83, 91; Michael Perez/AP Images, 84; Patrick Semansky/AP Images, 89; Oliver Contreras/Sipa USA/AP Images, 95

Editor: Arnold Ringstad
Series Designer: Becky Daum

Library of Congress Control Number: 2020951559

Publisher's Cataloging-in-Publication Data

Names: Murray, Laura K., author.
Title: Kamala Harris: first female US vice president / by Laura K. Murray
Other title: first female US vice president
Description: Minneapolis, Minnesota : Abdo Publishing, 2022 | Series: Essential Lives | Includes online resources and index.
Identifiers: ISBN 9781532195945 (lib. bdg.) | ISBN 9781098216719 (ebook)
Subjects: LCSH: Harris, Kamala, 1964---Juvenile literature. | Vice-Presidents--United States--Biography--Juvenile literature. | Women politicians--Biography--Juvenile literature. | African American women legislators--Biography--Juvenile literature. | Women legislators--United States--Biography--Juvenile literature.
Classification: DDC 328.73092--dc23

CONTENTS

CHAPTER 1
THE FIRST BUT NOT THE LAST   4

CHAPTER 2
**FROM CALIFORNIA
TO CANADA**   14

CHAPTER 3
LEARNING THE LAW   24

CHAPTER 4
AGAINST THE ODDS   32

CHAPTER 5
**CALIFORNIA'S
ATTORNEY GENERAL**   42

CHAPTER 6
SPEAKING UP IN THE SENATE   54

CHAPTER 7
RUNNING FOR PRESIDENT   64

CHAPTER 8
CALLS FOR JUSTICE   74

CHAPTER 9
MAKING HISTORY AGAIN   84

Timeline	96
Essential Facts	100
Glossary	102
Additional Resources	104
Source Notes	106
Index	110
About the Author	112
About the Consultant	112

CHAPTER ONE

THE FIRST BUT NOT THE LAST

It was one of the biggest moments of Kamala Harris's life. On the evening of November 7, 2020, Harris waited to enter the stage outside the Chase Center in Wilmington, Delaware, where she would make her victory speech. She had just been elected vice president of the United States. After her speech, Harris would introduce the president-elect, Joe Biden.

This was not a usual political rally with a crowd packed into an arena. With the COVID-19 pandemic ravaging the globe, the outdoor event was a drive-in rally. This allowed attendees to follow social distancing guidelines that were meant to help slow the spread of the disease. Still, excitement rippled through the air. Approximately 360 vehicles were parked in the brightly lit lot in front of the stage.[1] Supporters wore face coverings over their mouths and noses and sat inside, next to, and on top of cars decorated with Biden-Harris

Harris walked onstage to give her victory speech on the night of November 7. She wore a mask due to the deadly COVID-19 pandemic, removing it only during her speech.

signs. They held handmade posters and waved American flags, their cell phones ready to record. Thousands of additional supporters filled the surrounding streets.

Wearing a black face covering, Harris entered the flag-lined stage to the sounds of ecstatic cheers and blaring car horns. As she waved at the crowd, her image was projected on giant screens flanking the stage. Millions of viewers across the country watched the broadcast on television or streamed it live online. It was a milestone in Harris's own career, but it was also a historic moment for the United States. At age 56, Harris was set to become the first female vice president in the nation's history. She would also be the first Black person and first Asian American in the position. Being the daughter of immigrants set her apart from many of her predecessors as well. Her late mother, a breast

> ## VICE PRESIDENTIAL CANDIDATES
>
> In addition to Harris, two other women have been major-party nominees for the office of vice president. In 1984, Democratic nominee Geraldine Ferraro ran alongside Walter Mondale. They lost to Ronald Reagan and running mate George H. W. Bush. In 2008, Republican nominee Sarah Palin ran alongside John McCain. They lost to Barack Obama and running mate Joe Biden. In 2016, Democratic candidate Hillary Clinton became the first woman from a major political party to run for president. She lost to Donald Trump.

cancer researcher, was from India, while her father, an economist, was from Jamaica.

In her victory speech, Harris thanked the women who had come before her. She gave special recognition to her mother, Shyamala, who had been a shaping influence on her life. "I am thinking about her and about the generations of women, Black women, Asian, white, Latina, Native American women," Harris said, "who throughout our nation's history have paved the way for this moment tonight, women who fought and sacrificed

A CENTURY IN THE MAKING

Women's groups began their fight for suffrage, or the right to vote, in the 1840s. Over the following decades they used a variety of tactics, from demonstrations and picketing to hunger strikes and congressional lobbying. In August 1920, the US government ratified the Nineteenth Amendment to the US Constitution, giving US women the right to vote. However, in reality not all women were able to vote after the amendment's passage. Rules that made it difficult or impossible for women of color to vote remained in some states. The fight for suffrage for all women, including women of color and Native American women, would continue for decades.

When Harris became the first woman elected to the vice presidency in 2020, it marked 100 years since the ratification of the Nineteenth Amendment. Many observers speculated that Harris's white suit during her 2020 victory speech was a nod to past women activists, as the color has long been associated with suffragists. It has been worn on significant occasions by such leaders as Shirley Chisholm in 1968, Geraldine Ferraro in 1984, Hillary Clinton in 2016, and Democratic congresswomen in 2020.

so much for equality and liberty and justice for all."[2] Harris knew her election as vice president would help future generations see the possibility of achieving their own dreams. "While I may be the first woman in this office, I will not be the last," she said. This statement was based on her mother's advice, which had become something of a life motto for Harris. "You may be the first, but make sure you're not the last," Shyamala had told her daughter years before.[3]

Breaking Barriers

Harris was raised in California's Bay Area during the 1960s and 1970s. She received an early introduction to activism and social justice through her parents' involvement in the civil rights movement. Following her parents' divorce, Harris grew up with her mother and sister. During these years, she cultivated a sense of hard work, community, and fairness—and eventually an interest in the law as a way to help others.

After earning her law degree, Harris worked her way up as a prosecutor. Dealing with difficult cases made her determined to correct what she saw as disparities in the legal system and to bring justice to vulnerable people. At the Alameda County district attorney's other end of the political spectrum said she wasn't progressive enough. They accused her of supporting what they saw as unjust policies in the criminal justice system as attorney general. Some doubted her willingness to bring about real reform. Others questioned the consistency of her past positions on important issues.

That November night in Delaware, Harris's husband, Doug, joined her on the confetti-littered stage to wave at the crowd alongside Biden and his wife, Jill. Fireworks lit up the sky in celebration. As the divided nation stood on the verge of a new era, Harris knew the real work was just beginning, and all eyes were on her. Throughout her life, Harris had never backed down from a challenge. Once again, she found herself with something to prove.

THE FIRST SECOND GENTLEMAN

Harris's historic win as vice president created another first for the country. Harris's husband, Doug Emhoff, was poised to become the nation's first "second gentleman." A well-known lawyer, Emhoff planned to cut ties with his law firm before Harris's inauguration to avoid potential conflicts of interest. In late 2020, it was announced that Emhoff would teach an entertainment and media law course at Georgetown University's law school in the spring.

CHAPTER TWO

FROM CALIFORNIA TO CANADA

Kamala Devi Harris was born on October 20, 1964, at Kaiser Hospital in Oakland, California. Her first name, pronounced *comma-la*, is a traditional Indian name that means "lotus flower" in Sanskrit. Kamala's sister, Maya, was born two years after Kamala. The two remained close as they grew up.

Kamala's father, Donald Harris, was born in 1938 in Jamaica. He later immigrated to the United States to study economics at the University of California at Berkeley. Her mother, Shyamala Gopalan, was born in 1938 in southern India, the daughter of an Indian diplomat. At age 19, Shyamala immigrated to the United States to work toward a graduate degree at Berkeley. Shyamala had dreams of one day curing breast cancer. She and Donald met through their participation in the civil rights movement. They married in 1963. It was uncommon at the time for a young Indian woman to

California's Bay Area, including Oakland, was the site of protests and cultural upheaval during Harris's formative years there.

forgo an arranged marriage and instead strike out on her own in a new country, but Shyamala's parents were supportive. She earned her doctoral degree the same year Kamala was born.

As a girl, Kamala liked to sing, dance, and play outside. The family enjoyed music. Shyamala was a gifted singer, and Donald often played jazz albums from his collection. Kamala was also exposed to activism at an early age because of her parents' involvement in social justice and civil rights causes. "That's the language that I grew up hearing," she later recalled, "and it was about a belief that we are a country that was founded on noble ideals. And we are the best of who we are when we fight to achieve those ideals."[1] The Harrises brought their young children along to civil rights demonstrations, and Kamala came to think of

DONALD HARRIS

Kamala has spoken little about her father, Donald, a former economics professor at Stanford University. Media outlets have reported that Donald's relationship with his daughter is allegedly "strained" and pointed out that his name has been noticeably missing in Kamala's speeches recognizing her family.[2] In a 2018 essay for *Jamaica Global Online*, Donald wrote about the importance of instilling the family's Jamaican heritage in his daughters when they visited his home country as children. During the 2020 presidential campaign, Donald told the media he would not be doing interviews.

her parents' close friends, who were local community organizers, as aunts and uncles.

Looking Up to Shyamala

By the time Kamala was five years old, her parents had separated. They formally divorced when she was seven. While Kamala and Maya visited their father occasionally, they were mainly raised by their mother. "She was the one most responsible for shaping us into the women we would become," Kamala later wrote in her autobiography, *The Truths We Hold*.[3] Shyamala held her daughters to high standards and encouraged them to lift others up along the way. She also passed on her passion for justice, history, politics, and equality.

Shyamala, Kamala, and Maya moved to a duplex in west Berkeley in a predominantly Black area known as the flatlands. The area had a diverse population racially and economically. Kamala took dance and piano lessons, sang in the Baptist church choir, and sometimes went along to her mother's lab, where she helped clean test tubes and performed other small jobs. On school days, Kamala took the bus to Thousand Oaks Elementary School in north Berkeley. Kamala didn't know it at the time, but being bused to the elementary school across town was part of a project to desegregate schools. Kamala's beloved first-grade teacher, Frances Wilson, remained one of her lifelong supporters.

Learning by Example

In Berkeley, the trio found a welcoming community that knew them as "Shyamala and the girls."[4] A few houses down, the Shelton family ran a day care as well as an after-school program, which Kamala and Maya attended until their mother got home from work. Kamala was influenced by Regina Shelton's dedication to helping others. Shelton took in foster children and worked to improve the neighborhood. Kamala later referred to

BUSING DEBATE

The busing program that carried Kamala across Berkeley to Thousand Oaks Elementary was part of a hotly debated national experiment in desegregating schools. Some parents opposed the busing program. In Boston and other cities, violence erupted, and court-ordered busing experiments ended. However, in 1968, Berkeley voluntarily implemented a busing program, which became a model for other integration efforts across the country. In Berkeley's system, both Black and white students were bused to different neighborhoods. In 1963, Thousand Oaks Elementary had been 95 percent white and 3 percent Black. By the end of the decade, it was 53 percent white and 40 percent Black.[5] Kamala was part of Berkeley's second class to participate in the busing experiment. "At the time, all I knew was that the big yellow bus was the way I got to school," she later recalled.[6]

Busing desegregation programs were carried out across the country in the 1970s. In some places busing occurred peacefully, but in other cities there was intense opposition from white parents.

Mrs. Shelton as her second mother. Other neighbors and friends took care of each other and looked out for everyone's best interests. Living in Berkeley, Kamala saw that family friends who were lawyers were called on to help with all kinds of problems. "I wanted to be the one people called. I wanted to be the one who could help," she later said.[7]

Kamala and her sister were raised both Hindu and Baptist, with their mother instilling in them an appreciation for both their Indian and Black heritages. Shyamala took her daughters to visit India throughout their childhoods to ensure they kept in touch with their roots. Shyamala's father, P. V. Gopalan, was a longtime Indian civil servant. As a young girl, Kamala visited him and her grandmother, Rajam, in India as well as in Zambia, where they were working to help settle refugees. Seeing her family's work in public service left a lasting impression on Kamala.

Shyamala wanted her daughters to see themselves as proud Black women. In the Bay Area, Kamala found mentors and people who took pride in being Black. She was surrounded by positivity about Black culture, from the artists and thinkers who frequented the nearby Black cultural center to the posters of historical Black figures that hung on Mrs. Shelton's walls.

Moving to Canada

When Kamala was 12, her mother got a job at McGill University in Montreal, a major city in the Canadian province

---

THE RAINBOW SIGN

Growing up in Berkeley, Kamala was influenced by her visits to the Rainbow Sign, a Black cultural center. Founded by Mary Ann Pollar in 1971, the Rainbow Sign was a welcoming space for Black music, art, gatherings, and discussion. It soon became a Bay Area icon. Famous figures such as poet Maya Angelou and singer Nina Simone performed there. "I came to understand that there is no better way to feed someone's brain than by bringing together food, poetry, politics, music, dance, and art," Harris later said.[8]

of Quebec. Kamala and Maya were not excited to leave their beloved California for a distant French-speaking city. The move was a culture shock. Kamala only knew a few French terms from her ballet lessons, but classes were taught in French at her new school, Notre-Dame-des-Neiges (meaning "Our Lady of the Snows"). Later, Kamala persuaded her mother to let her enroll in a fine arts middle school instead.

Kamala continued to miss California but got settled into her new home. She also started putting into practice some of the lessons in activism that had been instilled in her. When she was 13, Kamala organized a group of fellow kids outside their apartment building to protest that they were not allowed to play soccer on the lawn. They got the rule changed. In the summers, Kamala returned to her home state, visiting her father or Mrs. Shelton.

At Quebec's diverse Westmount High School, Kamala shifted easily between the student groups of various backgrounds and interests. She cofounded an all-girl dance troupe called first the Super Six and later Midnight Magic. Dressed in homemade costumes, the group performed to disco grooves at school, fundraisers, and senior centers. Kamala graduated from the public high school in 1981.

Learning at Howard

Kamala wanted to return to the United States for college and was accepted to Howard University, a historically Black university in Washington, DC, where she majored in political science and economics. At Howard, Kamala found a supportive environment that encouraged students to live up to their potentials. In her first year, Kamala was elected student representative, participated in debate team, and chaired the economics society. She also became a member of the Alpha Kappa Alpha sorority, forging deep bonds with many of the women.

HISTORICALLY BLACK COLLEGES AND UNIVERSITIES

After the banning of slavery in the United States in 1865, Black Americans were still discriminated against in many areas of life, including education. Many institutions in Southern states did not allow any Black students to attend, while others only allowed a small number of Black students. As a result, historically Black colleges and universities (HBCUs) were created to educate mainly Black students. Established in 1867, Howard University is one of the oldest HBCUs in the country. School segregation was prohibited with the passage of the Civil Rights Act of 1964, but the legacy of HBCUs has continued. Today there are 101 HBCUs in the United States.

Kamala's family was growing around this time. In 1984, Kamala's niece, Meena, was born to Maya. Maya was a high school senior at the time, and she raised her daughter as a single mother.

During college, Kamala continued her involvement in civic engagement and social justice, participating in protests on issues such as apartheid in South Africa. She also gained valuable work experience, including an internship at the Federal Trade Commission and jobs at the National Archives and the US Bureau of Engraving and Printing. One summer, she interned with California senator Alan Cranston. When Kamala graduated in 1986, she was ready to change the world. The best way to do that, she figured, was through the political system—and a good route into politics was earning a law degree.

MAYA HARRIS

A graduate of Stanford Law School, Kamala's sister Maya has built a successful career in law, public policy, writing, and activism. She has held positions with the American Civil Liberties Union (ACLU) and the Ford Foundation and has directed efforts to address inequality in schools and the justice system. During the 2016 presidential campaign, she worked as a senior adviser to Hillary Clinton. She also chaired her sister's yearlong presidential bid in 2019. Kamala and Maya's relationship has prompted comparisons to that of President John F. Kennedy and his brother Robert Kennedy because of Maya's role as a loyal ally and confidante to her sister.

CHAPTER THREE

LEARNING THE LAW

After graduating from Howard, Harris returned to Oakland and enrolled at the University of California, Hastings College of the Law, located in San Francisco. Harris was part of the Legal Education Opportunity Program, which aimed to increase campus diversity. In her second year, she was elected president of the Black Law Students Association. In 1988, Harris did a summer internship in the Alameda County district attorney's office, also located in the Bay Area. The program was an important learning experience for Harris, introducing her to the real-life work of being a prosecutor. Only one other woman was part of the internship program, and the two struck up a friendship.

Over the summer, Harris got to observe many different cases, including one she later called "a defining moment" of her life.[1] In this case, a woman had been arrested after simply standing nearby during a drug bust. The matter would be easily cleared up, but the woman was to be held in jail until the judge heard the

Harris's time at Hastings gave her a great deal of new knowledge and experience.

case a few days later. Concerned about the ramifications for the innocent woman's family, children, and job, Harris convinced the judge to hear the case right away, and the woman was quickly released. Harris never met the woman, but she realized the difference she could make in someone's life by being his or her advocate. "It was a moment that proved how much it mattered to have compassionate people working as prosecutors. . . . and I knew the kind of work I wanted to do, and who I wanted to serve," she wrote in her autobiography.[2]

Harris graduated from Hastings in 1989. Along with her family, her first-grade teacher, Mrs. Wilson, was there at her graduation to support her. Harris passed the California bar examination the following year.

As Harris set out to be what she called a "progressive prosecutor," she had to defend her career choice to some.[3] Friends, family, and community members questioned why she wanted to work in a system they felt had historically treated

> **TRY, TRY AGAIN**
>
> In order to receive her license to practice law in California, Harris needed to pass the state's challenging bar exam. Harris was shocked when she received the test results back—she had failed. "I wondered if people thought I was a fraud," she later said. "But I held my head up."[4] She studied with renewed purpose and retook the exam a few months later, passing on her second attempt.

marginalized groups unfairly. Harris understood her community's doubts and had seen how the legal system could be used to perpetuate injustice. However, she was inspired by those who had used the justice system for good, correcting wrongs such as racial discrimination. She planned to offer her unique perspective and experiences to make decisions. She was determined to work within the system and change it for the better.

Jumping In at Alameda County

In 1990, Harris began working as deputy district attorney for Alameda County. She found herself on the front lines as a courtroom prosecutor and as a firsthand witness to both the faults and merits of the justice system. Harris quickly saw the effects of mass incarceration,

THURGOOD MARSHALL

Harris cites Thurgood Marshall (1908–1993) as one of her inspirations. A graduate of Howard University, Marshall was the first Black person to serve on the US Supreme Court. The Baltimore-born civil rights leader and lawyer spearheaded the push to end legal segregation in the United States. Before president Lyndon B. Johnson appointed him to the Supreme Court in 1967, Marshall argued landmark cases before the court, including 1954's *Brown v. Board of Education*, in which the court unanimously ruled that segregation in public schools was unconstitutional. But even after the ruling, particularly in the South, white citizens and officials resisted desegregation.

or jailing large numbers of people. People who were arrested for small drug offenses often found it impossible to escape the cycle of drugs, gangs, crime, and prison. Researchers have found that mass incarceration disproportionately affects Black and Hispanic Americans. "In the rush to clean up the streets, we were criminalizing a public health crisis," she later said.[5]

As Harris worked her way through cases of lower-level crime, her responsibilities grew to include more serious cases. She eventually specialized in cases of child sexual assault as well as homicide and robbery. Throughout her time at Alameda County, she dealt with hundreds of cases. She interviewed witnesses, reviewed police reports, examined autopsy photos, visited jails and hospitals, and rushed to crime scenes in the middle of the night. Harris later recalled the difficulty of working on such intense cases, particularly crimes against children and cases in which sexual assault survivors were not believed. The stories of survivors would stay with her for years afterward.

Climbing the Ranks

In 1998, Harris took a job in the San Francisco district attorney's office, which was led by Terence

As deputy district attorney for Alameda County, Harris gained direct experience with the legal system.

Hallinan. There, she managed the Career Criminal Unit and oversaw a team of prosecutors. Her cases included those of serial violent offenders as well as so-called "three strikes" cases. Under California law,

> **THREE STRIKES**
>
> In 1994, California voters overwhelmingly passed the state's three strikes law following highly publicized murders. Meant to keep violent criminals off the streets, the law was controversial for its harsh punishments. The majority of people sentenced under the law were serving sentences for nonviolent crimes. A decade after it was passed, statistics from the California Department of Corrections showed that the three strikes law disproportionately affected minorities. More than 45 percent of people serving life sentences as a result of the law were Black.[6] In 2012, voters passed the Three Strikes Reform Act, which lessened the punishment for nonviolent crimes and created a process for current inmates to petition for a reduced sentence.

people could be sentenced to 25 years to life in prison for committing a third felony, violent or not—their third strike. Soon Harris became the chief of the Community and Neighborhood Division.

In 2000, San Francisco city attorney Louise Renne offered Harris a job at her office. Renne was the first woman in her position, and she welcomed Harris aboard to lead the office's Division on Families and Children. Harris was passionate about working on policies that would address foster care issues, juvenile crimes, and child abuse.

During this time, Harris helped establish a task force that focused on assisting sexually exploited youth in San Francisco. From her experience as a prosecutor, she believed youth who were being prostituted should be treated as victims who needed help rather than criminals who needed to be punished. The task force found success in securing funding and resources to help exploited youth. For Harris, it was fulfilling to have an integral role in large-scale changes. She decided her next move would be running for elected office.

COMBATING EXPLOITATION AND TRAFFICKING

Throughout her career, Harris has worked to combat exploitation and human trafficking. When Harris worked in the San Francisco city attorney's office, she helped establish a task force to address youth sexual exploitation. The group included survivors as well as experts and community members. The task force recommended shelters, resources, and treatments for exploited youth to get the help they needed. The recommendations were accepted and funded by the city's board of supervisors. This resulted in San Francisco's first safe house for sexually exploited youth.

Harris also worked on this issue by supporting legislation such as the California Trafficking Victims Protection Act. Signed into law in 2005, it made human trafficking a felony in the state. She also advocated legislation for tougher penalties for child sex crimes and created San Francisco's unit dedicated to handling child sexual assault cases. Harris later served on the California Alliance to Combat Trafficking and Slavery Task Force. She was also chosen to cochair the California District Attorneys Association's Sex Crimes Committee. In 2012, she sponsored a bill that prevented human traffickers from benefiting financially from their crimes. Another bill would help victims receive restitution.

CHAPTER FOUR

AGAINST THE ODDS

Harris first ran for elected office in 2003, entering the race for district attorney of San Francisco. It seemed like a long shot. "A lot of people told her not to run," recalled Democratic strategist Debbie Mesloh, who is a friend of Harris's.[1] The city was in the midst of turbulence, with ongoing investigations into alleged city corruption and police cover-ups. Harris would be going up against the current district attorney, Terence Hallinan—her former boss and a well-known figure who was also running on a progressive platform.

Undeterred, Harris entered the race with the message that she was not only progressive but also capable and more effective in curbing crime. She utilized the network of contacts that she had built in her law career and secured supporters to help fund her campaign. One campaign advertisement she mailed showed photos of former San Francisco district attorneys—all white men. The text read, "It's time for a change."[2] She knocked on doors, stood outside grocery

Harris talks with supporters while campaigning for the San Francisco district attorney job.

stores, and waited at bus stops in attempts to engage potential voters. Boosted by an endorsement by the *San Francisco Chronicle*, Harris inched upward in the polls.

Finally, the election arrived. When no candidate received a majority of the vote, the election went to a runoff between the top two candidates. With 56.5 percent of the vote, Harris achieved victory, becoming the first woman and person of color to be San Francisco's district attorney.[3] She was also the first Black woman and first South Asian woman to be a district attorney anywhere in the state of California. At her swearing-in ceremony, her mother stood by her side.

Under Fire

In her new role, Harris's decision-making skills were quickly put to the test. On April 10, 2004, 29-year-old San Francisco police officer Isaac Espinoza was shot and killed by a 21-year-old gang member. Harris, who had run on an anti–death penalty campaign promise, did not pursue the death penalty against Espinoza's killer, instead seeking a sentence of life imprisonment without parole. She received public backlash and criticism from police officers, who saw her stance as a lack of support

Shyamala held a copy of the Bill of Rights at Harris's swearing-in ceremony.

for law enforcement. However, Harris's supporters applauded her for standing by her campaign pledge.

Harris attended Espinoza's funeral, where US senator for California Dianne Feinstein gave the eulogy for the officer, who was survived by his wife and three-year-old daughter. In her speech, Feinstein questioned the decision of not seeking the death penalty, spurring a standing ovation by hundreds of officers in attendance as they turned to face Harris. Although other leaders such as Senator Barbara Boxer, Oakland mayor Jerry Brown, and police groups pressured Harris to reverse course, she refused to change her decision. As a result of the case, police groups withheld their support from Harris for years to come.

Back on Track

As district attorney, one of Harris's priorities was breaking the cycle of crime. She disagreed with mass incarcerations of low-level drug offenders. Prisons were overcrowded, and taxpayers were bearing the burden of housing inmates. Part of the problem stemmed from low-level drug offenders ending up back in prison after being released. Harris believed that low-level drug offenders were less likely to be incarcerated again if they had basic skills and a plan before they reentered the community.

In 2005, Harris tapped civil rights activist Lateefah Simon to help create the San Francisco Reentry Division, which created a program called Back on

---

HINDSIGHT

Years later, Harris stood by her decision in the case of Officer Isaac Espinoza, but she conceded that she might have handled it differently. In particular, she said she may have waited until after the funeral to announce the charges that her office would be pursuing. "Maybe it was a political novice mistake. I don't know," she told the *San Francisco Chronicle* in 2019. "Maybe it was the right thing to do, but you got to take the heat for it."[4]

Part of Harris's role as district attorney was speaking to the media about high-profile cases.

Track. Back on Track gave first-time nonviolent drug offenders ages 18 to 30 an alternative to jail. As part of the program, defendants had to get educated, hold a job, report regularly to a judge, take drug tests, and show responsibility. Those that followed through with the yearlong program had their felony charge removed from their records.

The Back on Track program saw positive results. Four years after launching, it reported that repeat offenses occurred with less than 10 percent of its graduates, compared with more than 50 percent of those who didn't go through the program. It had also saved San Francisco approximately $2 million per year in jail costs and other expenses.[5] Other cities and states would later use Back on Track as a template for their own programs.

Rising Recognition

Harris made moves to further other key causes. She established a hate crimes unit that focused on addressing anti-LGBTQ violence and called on lawmakers and prosecutors to stop using the "gay panic" or "trans panic"

GAY/TRANS PANIC DEFENSE

As district attorney, Harris was horrified by the use of the "gay panic" or "trans panic" defense. This refers to defendants claiming that sexual advances by gay or trans people triggered a violent reaction, excusing the defendant's crimes. Those using the tactic often blame the victim's sexual orientation or identity for causing the defendant to panic or go temporarily insane. In 2002, this defense made headlines when four men brutally murdered transgender teen Gwen Araujo in California.

Harris set out to eliminate the defense, bringing together law enforcement and prosecutors for a national conference to discuss the issue. She continued working to abolish the gay/trans panic defense later in her career. Under her leadership, California became the first state to ban the practice by law in 2014. In 2019, Senator Edward Markey and Representative Joseph Kennedy III reintroduced a bill to prohibit the defense federally. In 2020, a handful of states had banned the gay/trans panic defense.

defense. This defense was used in cases where people attacked LGBTQ people and claimed that this violence was justified because the LGBTQ victim's identity spooked the attacker. Harris felt this idea excused violence against LGBTQ people.

Harris also addressed climate change, establishing the district attorney office's first environmental justice unit. She pushed back against the state's three strikes policy, requiring that her office charge for the third strike penalty only if the felony was a serious or violent crime. Harris also significantly increased felony conviction rates, including more than doubling the rates for felony gun trials. She also focused on the issue of school truancy, stating that high school dropouts were more likely to be involved in crimes or be victims of crimes. To combat truancy, she began filing charges against parents of children who consistently missed

ENVIRONMENTAL JUSTICE

When Harris established California's first environmental justice unit in 2005, it was focused on the fact that environmental crimes disproportionately affect people in poverty. It looked to combat actions such as dumping waste illegally, operating in unsanitary conditions, polluting areas near neighborhoods, and creating hazards for residents. "The people who live in those communities often have no other choice but to live there," Harris said at the time.[6]

school. Critics accused the measures of being too punitive and contributing to the cycle of jail time for nonviolent offenses. Harris's anti-truancy efforts would remain controversial throughout her career.

People were taking notice of the district attorney. In 2005, Harris received the Thurgood Marshall Award, named for one of her heroes, from the National Black Prosecutors Association, and she appeared on *Newsweek*'s list of most powerful women. Her alma mater, Howard University, recognized her as one of its Outstanding Alumni. Harris won reelection as San Francisco district attorney in 2007, running unopposed. The following year, she announced she would run for attorney general of California in 2010. In 2009, Harris published her first book, *Smart on Crime: A Career Prosecutor's Plan to Make Us Safer*, which explained

> **THE BUCK STOPS HERE**
>
> Harris's critics have called into question her inaction in a controversial 2009 incident in which a crime lab technician stole cocaine from the lab. Harris's office did not inform defense attorneys of the incident, which could have affected the rights of their clients. As a result, an estimated 1,000 drug-related cases had to be thrown out.[7] Later, Harris said she had not been aware of the actions that her office had taken but took responsibility for the scandal nonetheless. "The bottom line is the buck stops with me, and I take full responsibility for what my office did," she said.[8]

her ideas on how prosecutors and lawmakers should work on criminal justice reforms while remaining tough on crime.

Personal Heartbreak

Meanwhile, Harris was dealing with devastating personal news. In 2008, her mother was diagnosed with colon cancer. Harris took her mother to chemotherapy treatments, cooked her meals, and helped care for her as her condition worsened. Shyamala had been a steady presence during campaigning and at community events, supporting her daughter in her elected role. Now as Harris watched her mother battle the illness, she struggled to come to terms with losing her most ardent supporter.

Shyamala died on February 11, 2009. She was 70 years old. Harris brought her mother's ashes to Chennai, India, where Shyamala was born. Harris scattered the ashes in the Indian Ocean. Wherever life took her next, Harris would never forget the values her mother had instilled in her.

CHAPTER FIVE

CALIFORNIA'S ATTORNEY GENERAL

The 2010 race for California attorney general was Harris's biggest stage yet. Once again, she was the underdog. The attorney general is the top law enforcement official in the state, and California was the largest state in the nation by population. Unlike most of California's statewide races, which generally favored Democratic candidates, the attorney general race would be a hard-fought battle. Even people in Harris's own party were skeptical of her chances. Democratic strategist Garry South remarked that Harris's status as "a woman, who is a minority, who is anti–death penalty, who is district attorney of wacky San Francisco" would hurt her electability.[1] After making it through the primary, she faced well-known Los Angeles county district attorney Steve Cooley in the general election.

Harris and her campaign team opened a field office in Los Angeles in order to target that county's voters.

Harris speaks during a debate with her Republican opponent, Los Angeles district attorney Steve Cooley, in October 2010.

Her campaign was boosted by support from Black voter registration groups, labor unions, and other groups. She also received a key endorsement from President Barack Obama. However, the Cooley campaign accused Harris of being soft on crime, pointing to her refusal to seek the death penalty in the 2004 murder of Officer Espinoza. Harris defended her record, saying, "I will not cede my law enforcement and crime fighting credentials to anyone. There are a whole lot of people spending a whole lot of time in state prison because of work I've personally done in the courtroom."[2]

As expected, the vote on election night was close—so close that Harris and her team couldn't believe it when Cooley delivered a victory speech that evening. A San Francisco newspaper also reported that Cooley had won. However, votes were still being counted, and Harris was pulling

NOT THE FEMALE OBAMA

Harris and Barack Obama met in 2004 when Obama ran for Senate, and she endorsed him during his 2008 presidential run. Throughout Harris's career, some media outlets referred to her as "the female Obama" because of certain similarities in their background and personalities.[3] Critics of the description point out that it minimizes Harris's own accomplishments. When Harris was once asked about carrying on Obama's legacy, she replied, "I have my own legacy."[4]

ahead. In the end, Harris won 46.1 percent of the votes to Cooley's 45.3 percent.[5] Harris was named the winner, becoming the first Black person and first woman to serve as California's attorney general.

On January 3, 2011, she took the oath of office as attorney general. Her sister, Maya, stood beside her for the swearing-in ceremony, holding a Bible that belonged to Mrs. Shelton, their "second mother" from Berkeley.[6] Harris got to work with the knowledge that she could make her biggest impact yet. However, the high-profile position also opened her up for more criticism than ever. Throughout her tenure as attorney general, she made waves, garnering supporters and detractors alike. She would go on to win reelection in 2014.

Getting to Work

Harris's work with controversial anti-truancy policies continued as attorney general. In 2011, a state law that she had worked on went into effect. The law

DEFYING EXPECTATIONS

Harris's victory in the 2010 California attorney general race took even her staff by surprise. "History was against her," her campaign manager, Brian Brokaw, later recalled to RollCall.com. "The electoral dynamic was against her. Everybody just assumed that the Democrats [were] going to win all the statewide races, except for that one. . . . That was the conventional wisdom, and she defied it."[7]

Harris gave her first press conference as attorney general–elect on November 30, 2010.

made it possible to charge a misdemeanor to parents of children who missed more than 10 percent of school days without a valid excuse. The parents could receive a fine or up to one year of jail time. In her inauguration address, Harris said she was putting parents on notice. "If you fail in your responsibility to your kids, we are going to work to make sure you face the full force and consequences of the law," she stated.[8] Critics said the law served to unfairly punish people of color and families that were dealing with circumstances such as illnesses, poverty, and lack of transportation.

Critics pointed to inconsistencies in her record. Harris said she personally opposed the death penalty, and she had refused to seek it as district attorney in the Espinoza case, but she didn't support ballot initiatives to ban the death penalty in California. Some progressives accused her of maintaining the status quo rather than being proactive in ending the death penalty.

Harris continued addressing criminal justice issues. In 2013, she established a division of the California Department of Justice dedicated to aiding the reentry

CHALLENGING TRUANCY

The goal of Harris's anti-truancy efforts was to increase interventions and consequences so that parents would ensure their children were in school. Supporters attested that the crackdown would lessen criminal activity and improve children's educations. However, the efforts have long been a sticking point among progressives, who say the policies unnecessarily prosecuted parents, particularly minorities and low-income people, for circumstances beyond their control. They argued Harris should have instead focused on addressing larger social problems.

In one case, parent Cheree Peoples was arrested at her home in Orange County in 2013. Her daughter, Shayla, had a genetic illness that caused her to regularly miss school. Peoples was led outside in handcuffs in front of news crews. After two years of living what Peoples called a "nightmare" of court cases, the charges were dismissed.[9] Critics pointed to such cases as proof of the harmful effects of anti-truancy efforts. In 2019, Harris said the intention of the policies was never to criminalize parents. Journalists at the *Los Angeles Times* and elsewhere have noted that Harris's stance on truancy has shifted over the years from a punishment-based approach to a more tolerant stance—a shift that has reflected similar shifts in public opinion.

of former inmates into society and reducing the rate of repeat offenders. She partnered with district attorney offices in Alameda County, Los Angeles, and San Diego for the initiative. In 2015, she expanded the Back on Track program in partnership with the Los Angeles County Sheriff's Department.

Other efforts focused on increasing transparency and reducing racial bias in policing. In 2015, she launched the OpenJustice data platform, which provides law enforcement data to the public. It includes metrics on deaths in custody, arrests, bookings, and other statistics. Soon after, Harris offered implicit bias training courses for police officers, which were meant to show officers how they may act on attitudes or stereotypes unintentionally and give them ways to reduce that bias. The trainings were meant to foster trust between police and the communities they serve. Still, Harris received criticism for not doing enough to reform the criminal justice system.

Big Wins

As attorney general, Harris made her mark in fighting fraud against the government through California's False Claims Act. In one such case in 2011, she recovered

The police chief of Stockton, California, speaks alongside Harris and other law enforcement officials at a 2015 news conference about implicit bias training.

$241 million for taxpayers in a case against a medical testing company that had committed fraud.[10] It was the largest recovery under the law in the state's history.

In another landmark case, she took on the country's five largest mortgage firms, which were accused of illegally foreclosing on homeowners. Many Californians had been affected. Going into negotiations with the mortgage firms in September 2011, Harris felt the weight of the constituents who were relying on her. When the banks offered only $2 billion to

$4 billion dollars to Californians, Harris decided to pull out of negotiations. It was a risky move, and Harris knew there was a lot at stake. But she also thought the offer didn't properly cover the damages. "This was about trying to get justice for millions of people who needed and deserved help," she later said.[11] She held firm to her decision. Harris prevailed, and the settlement eventually reached $18 billion for Californians.[12] In 2012, Harris worked with lawmakers to pass the Homeowner Bill of Rights, which gave protections to homeowners facing foreclosure.

Other big cases were in areas ranging from consumer protection to big tech. In 2015, Harris won a case against Corinthian Colleges for more than $1 billion. The for-profit college was found to have targeted low-income, vulnerable people with false advertising and claims, leaving students with massive debt. "For years, Corinthian profited off the backs of poor people—now they have to pay," Harris said in a statement. "This judgment sends a clear message: there is a cost to this kind of predatory conduct."[13] Harris also launched cases against large technology firms, including Google, for not protecting consumer privacy. Meanwhile, she established the California Department

During a press conference, Harris gestures to a table full of counterfeit jewelry seized from online sellers.

of Justice's eCrime Unit to address identity theft and other technology-related crimes.

Harris also continued to defend LGBTQ rights. In 2008, California voters passed Proposition 8, which declared marriage to be between a man and a woman. However, as attorney general, Harris refused to defend Proposition 8, arguing that it was unconstitutional. Governor Jerry Brown also refused to defend it. After Proposition 8 was ruled unconstitutional in district court, the case went to the US Supreme Court. However, the Supreme Court ruled that Proposition 8 proponents could not legally defend the law in federal court. This affirmed the district court's ruling that Proposition 8 was unconstitutional. On June 28, 2013,

Harris officiated California's first same-sex wedding after the decision, performing the marriage of two of the plaintiffs in the Supreme Court case, Kris Perry and Sandy Stier of Berkeley. In her time as attorney general, Harris also established an LGBT Victim Advocacy Unit and an LGBT Sexual Assault Awareness Program.

Fighting for Justice

Harris's office brought charges against criminals who used the internet for trafficking and exploitation. In 2015, Harris established the Bureau of Children's Justice (BCJ). Among its main focuses were issues within foster care systems, discrimination in education, human trafficking of youth, and homelessness affecting children.

In 2012, Harris signed an agreement with Mexico's attorney general, Marisela

SHUTTING DOWN BACKPAGE

Harris made national headlines in 2016 when, alongside Texas attorney general Ken Paxton, she announced the raid of a well-known online advertising company called Backpage and the arrest of its CEO. Following a three-year investigation and undercover operations, Harris's office charged him with felonies related to the prostitution of minors. Harris said that the website's online ads included child victims of human trafficking. The CEO eventually pleaded guilty to various charges in 2018, including human trafficking.

Morales, to better coordinate law enforcement against gangs at the California–Mexico border. Harris also brought charges against drug cartels for crimes involving human trafficking, drugs, weapons, money laundering, and technology. Her office also carried out raids on various gangs.

From Kamala to "Momala"

With Harris's national profile on the rise, she was named one of *Time* magazine's 100 most influential people in 2014. That same year, she married entertainment and media lawyer Doug Emhoff. The two had met in 2013 on a blind date. They were married on August 22, 2014, at the Santa Barbara courthouse. Harris's sister, Maya, officiated the small ceremony, which included elements of the bride and groom's Indian and Jewish traditions, respectively.

Harris became stepmother to Doug's two children, Cole and Ella, from his prior marriage to film producer Kerstin Emhoff. Rather than use the term *stepmom*, Cole and Ella called Kamala "Momala."[14] Having Sunday night dinner together became an important routine for the family to spend time together during their busy weeks.

CHAPTER SIX

SPEAKING UP IN THE SENATE

In 2015, Harris decided to run for US Senate in the following year's election after longtime senator Barbara Boxer's seat opened up. Harris received endorsements from President Barack Obama, Vice President Joe Biden, and California governor Jerry Brown. The general election did not include a Republican candidate. Instead, Harris ran against Democratic congresswoman Loretta Sanchez. Harris won the election by a landslide, becoming the junior senator from California. She was the second Black woman and first South Asian American to be elected in Senate history.

Despite her own victory, Harris remained focused on the results of the race for the US presidency. Republican candidate Donald Trump had defeated Democratic candidate Hillary Clinton in a race that had highlighted divisions in the country. Harris strongly disagreed with

Harris greets people phone banking for her campaign in the summer of 2016.

Trump's rhetoric about women, immigrants, the press, and other groups. "Do we retreat or do we fight?" she asked in her acceptance speech. "I say we fight. And I intend to fight."[1]

Harris was poised to confront the new administration. Two days after her election, she made her first public remarks as senator-elect from outside the Coalition for Humane Immigrant Rights in Los Angeles. During his campaign, Trump had called for mass deportations, the construction of a border wall between the United States and Mexico, and the cancellation of policies such as Deferred Action for Childhood Arrivals (DACA), which protected people who had been brought to the United States illegally as children. As the daughter of immigrants, immigration was a personal issue for Harris.

CAROL MOSELEY BRAUN

Carol Moseley Braun was the first Black woman to be elected to the US Senate, serving from 1993 to 1999. After working as a prosecutor, she served in the Illinois House of Representatives before being elected as a US senator for Illinois. Throughout her career, Moseley Braun advocated for social reforms and spoke out on issues affecting women, children, and people of color. She served as US ambassador to New Zealand and Samoa from 1999 to 2001. In 2004, she launched an unsuccessful bid for the Democratic nomination for president.

Flanked by immigrants and activists, Harris criticized Trump's immigration policies and vowed to take action. "Today we are rededicating ourselves to fighting for the best of who we are. And there are a lot of people, as a result of this election, that are feeling dispirited at best," she said. "Part of what we have to say is that you are not alone, you matter, and we've got your back."[2]

Making Waves

On January 3, 2017, outgoing vice president Biden swore in Harris as a US senator. Cole was attending college, and Ella was starting her senior year of high school in Los Angeles. Harris knew it was going to be difficult to be away from her family, but her Senate job required her to be in Washington, particularly because she held positions on Senate committees that dealt with classified information. She joined the Homeland Security and Governmental Affairs Committee, the Select Committee on Intelligence, the Committee on the Judiciary, and the Committee on the Budget.

On January 21, 2017, Harris joined activists and lawmakers speaking to the 200,000 demonstrators gathered for the Women's March on Washington in

Harris was a prominent speaker at the 2017 Women's March.

Washington, DC. Upwards of three million people around the country, and more around the globe, were joining in protests against the Trump presidency.[3] In Harris's speech, she said that women should be involved in tackling all the major issues the country faced, including reproductive rights, the economy, security, health care, climate change, and immigration. "It's going to be harder before it gets easier. I know we will rise to the challenge and I know we will keep fighting no matter what," she said. "Let's buckle in because it's going to be a bumpy ride."[4]

Harris quickly gained a reputation as a major critic of the Trump administration's policies. In March 2017, Trump signed Executive Order 13769. With a stated purpose of keeping out terrorists, the order banned people from seven predominantly Muslim countries from coming into the United States. It also suspended all entry of refugees into the country. The order was widely criticized by human rights groups and prompted protests and legal challenges.

When the order went into effect, Harris received an onslaught of calls from civil rights lawyers she had previously worked with. They were concerned that US Immigration and Customs Enforcement (ICE) was detaining people and not letting them speak to their attorneys. Harris called Secretary of Homeland Security John Kelly at home to find out what was going on. According to reports, Kelly never got back to her. Soon after, Harris introduced the Access to Counsel Act, her first Senate bill, which would prohibit federal officials from denying access to a lawyer for a person who is detained trying to reach the United States. The bill passed the House of Representatives in 2020, but it was not signed into law.

Sharp Questions

As a member of the Judiciary and Intelligence committees, Harris's exchanges with Trump nominees and top officials created a buzz as she used her experience as a prosecutor to ask pointed questions. In 2017, US attorney general Jeff Sessions came in front of the Intelligence Committee regarding his communications with Russian officials during the 2016 presidential campaign. After Harris asked Sessions several questions looking for a clear response, Sessions replied, "I'm not able to be rushed this fast. It makes me nervous."[5] The clip quickly went viral.

In 2018, Harris made waves in her questioning of Trump's Supreme Court nominee Brett Kavanaugh, pressing him on reproductive rights. She also gained attention with her focused questioning of US attorney general William Barr on the findings of Special Counsel Robert Mueller. Mueller had been appointed to investigate Russian interference in the 2016 election. At one point, Harris told Barr, "I think you've made it clear, sir, that you have not looked at the evidence and we can move on."[6] Some people criticized Harris's style of questioning. President Trump described her as "extraordinarily nasty" during the Kavanaugh confirmation hearing.[7] Meanwhile, supporters praised her forcefulness.

Taking Action

As a senator, Harris introduced various pieces of legislation, including bipartisan bills. In 2018, alongside Democratic senator Cory Booker of New Jersey and Republican senator Tim Scott of South Carolina, Harris

DETENTION CENTERS

President Trump introduced a zero tolerance policy on prosecuting immigrants at the Mexican border. This was intended to deter people from entering the country illegally. It also had the effect of separating children and their parents when the parents were detained. As a senator, Harris called for an end to the policy. In 2018, after touring an immigrant detention center near San Diego, California, Harris said she was "deeply disturbed" at the conditions and what she was told by mothers who were being detained. "This is contrary to the principles we hold dear," Harris said. "All suffered sex abuse and domestic violence, and fled for the safety of their children. My heart is broken. . . . Let's keep being their voice."[8]

A few months later, Immigration and Customs Enforcement (ICE) officials appeared in front of the Senate Homeland Security and Governmental Affairs Committee. Harris highlighted reports that children in detention centers had limited access to food and water and were mistreated in other ways as well. She questioned the officials on their comparison of detention centers with summer camps and pressed them on the number of families that had been separated.

> ## ANTI-LYNCHING LEGISLATION
>
> In 2020, the House passed a similar version of the Justice for the Victims of Lynching Act called the Emmett Till Antilynching Act. It was named for 14-year-old Emmett Till, a Black teen from Chicago who was brutally killed in Mississippi in 1955. Till had been murdered for allegedly flirting with a white woman. Republican senator Rand Paul of Kentucky objected to the Emmett Till Antilynching Act, wanting to narrow its definition of lynching because he thought the bill might lead to overly long sentences for crimes that didn't warrant them. He stalled the bill in the Senate.

introduced the Justice for the Victims of Lynching Act. The bill would make lynching a federal hate crime. "We finally have a chance to speak the truth about our past, and make clear that these hateful acts should never happen again without serious, severe, and swift consequence and accountability," Harris said.[9] The bill passed unanimously in the Senate, the first time the body had passed anti-lynching legislation after more than 200 attempts.[10] However, the bill was stalled in the House and did not move forward.

In 2017, Harris joined with Republican senator Rand Paul of Kentucky to introduce a bill that encouraged states to reform or eliminate bail systems, which keep people in jail while awaiting trial unless they can afford to pay bail. She also joined with senators from both parties to cosponsor a bill on election cybersecurity. The following year, Harris voted to approve the First Step Act, which addressed federal criminal justice reform. She also supported bills to legalize and decriminalize marijuana.

In November 2017, Harris traveled to Puerto Rico after Hurricane Maria wreaked havoc there. She became a vocal proponent of relief efforts. She also criticized what she saw as a lack of action from the Trump administration in response to the disaster. "The government failed Puerto Rico at every level in the wake of Hurricane Maria," she wrote.[11] She said that one of the failings was an inability to determine the death toll for the hurricane. In 2018, Harris sponsored a bill that would fund improvements in the government's analysis of natural disasters. However, the bill did not attract bipartisan support and did not move forward.

COMMENCEMENT ADDRESS

In 2017, Harris returned to Howard University to give the commencement address to new graduates. She called on them to make a difference. "You can march for Black lives on the street, and you can ensure law enforcement accountability by serving as a prosecutor or on a police commission," she said. "The reality is, on most matters, somebody is going to make the decision—so why not let it be you?"[12]

CHAPTER SEVEN

RUNNING FOR PRESIDENT

On Martin Luther King Jr. Day, January 21, 2019, Harris appeared on the TV show *Good Morning America* to announce she was running for president of the United States. "I love my country, and this is a moment in time that I feel a sense of responsibility to fight for the best of who we are," she said.[1]

With her sister, Maya, at the helm as campaign chair, Harris and her team set up their headquarters in Baltimore, Maryland, with a second office in Oakland. Her campaign slogan was "For the People." Harris held her first campaign rally in her hometown of Oakland before an enthusiastic crowd of more than 20,000 supporters.[2] She said that a return to decency and respect was needed. She said her positions on women's rights, immigration, national security, freedom of the press, and other issues were in opposition to

---

Harris held her first presidential rally on January 27, 2019, in front of Oakland's city hall.

the Trump administration's policies. In her campaign, Harris said her presidential administration would broaden health insurance coverage, invest in clean energy, and form closer ties with allies around the world.

Although the 2020 presidential election was nearly 22 months away, several other Democratic hopefuls were already looking to take on President Trump. The slate of candidates included New York senator Kirsten Gillibrand, Massachusetts senator Elizabeth Warren, and former Secretary of Housing and Urban Development Julián Castro. In the following months, the Democratic field became increasingly crowded, eventually reaching more than 20 candidates. Among them were former

CHANNELING CHISHOLM

Harris's red-and-yellow campaign logo paid tribute to a woman whose leadership paved the way for others. Shirley Chisholm, the first Black woman in Congress as well as the first woman and Black person to seek a presidential nomination for a major political party, had used a similar design on her campaign buttons in 1972. Harris has also quoted Chisholm's feminist slogan, "unbought and unbossed," and Chisholm's recommendation, "If they don't give you a seat at the table, bring a folding chair."[3] A New York native born in 1924, Chisholm highlighted social issues and civil rights in her campaigning. She received sexist attacks from critics and the media, including mainstream news articles criticizing her physical appearance, but she persevered.

vice president Biden, Vermont senator Bernie Sanders, Minnesota senator Amy Klobuchar, New Jersey senator Cory Booker, entrepreneur Andrew Yang, billionaire Mike Bloomberg, and the mayor of South Bend, Indiana, Pete Buttigieg.

Democratic Debates

A key moment for the Harris campaign came on June 27, 2019, when the senator joined other candidates from her party for the first Democratic debate in Miami. Going into the debate, Biden was considered the front-runner. Harris knew the event was an opportunity to differentiate herself and show the millions of Americans watching why she should be president. During the debate, Harris confronted Biden over his recent comments about his past relationships with segregation-supporting senators. She also noted his opposition to federally mandated busing for racial integration when he was a Delaware senator in the 1970s. Harris said that she didn't believe Biden was racist but that his comments were hurtful. "There was a little girl in California who was part of the second class to integrate her public schools. And she was bused

From left to right, Andrew Yang, Pete Buttigieg, Joe Biden, and Bernie Sanders were among Harris's many rivals for the Democratic nomination.

to school every day," Harris said. "And that little girl was me."[4]

Labeled a "blistering ambush" by *Politico*, the sharp exchange quickly went viral.[5] The Harris campaign team capitalized on the momentum, tweeting a photo of Harris as a child and selling T-shirts of the image. Following the debate, Harris received a large boost in the polls and saw a fundraising surge of approximately $3.2 million.[6] Some Democrats, including former senator Chris Dodd, criticized Harris's debate exchange with Biden for being a cheap attack. However, Harris's supporters, including her online fan base, leaped to her defense. Some said the criticism was an example of women being treated differently from men, while others said it demonstrated efforts to block her from the nomination. Harris participated in five Democratic debates in total.

Facing Attacks

Throughout the campaign, Harris was targeted with attacks based on her sex and race. One conspiracy theory that spread online suggested that Harris had reached elected office only because she was in a relationship with a California politician in the 1990s. At various points, other people called into question her eligibility to serve, suggesting that she might not have been born in the United States and therefore could not be president. President Trump amplified those claims. Observers pointed out that many of the attacks leveled at Harris regarding her ethnicity and immigrant parents were similar to the false attacks once used against Barack Obama.

ABUZZ WITH THE KHIVE

Harris's online fan base, the KHive, first appeared in 2017, as supporters began using the name in reference to the fan base of singer Beyoncé, which is known as the Beyhive. The phrase caught on, with passionate supporters using the hashtag #KHive to lend their enthusiasm to Harris's campaign and defend Harris against attacks. Even after Harris withdrew from the presidential race, the KHive lived on as what one member called "a digital army."[7]

Harris's Democratic rivals condemned the racist attacks. Harris, however, didn't let the accusations deter her. She told the Associated Press that she knew running for president was not going to be easy. "But I know if I'm not on the stage, there's a certain voice that will not be present on that stage. Knowing that there is a perspective, there is a life experience, there is a vision that must be heard and seen and present on that stage, and that I have an ability to do that."[8]

Meanwhile, conflict was brewing in the Senate. Harris was among the senators calling for Congress to impeach President Trump following the report released by Special Counsel Robert Mueller's investigation into Russian

ADDRESSING CRITICS

During Harris's run for president, she continued to contend with questions and criticism over her record as attorney general. Although Harris has described herself as a progressive prosecutor, activists said she didn't do enough to reform the criminal justice system. "Harris . . . allowed many parts of the Justice Department to essentially operate as they long had, which at times led to what many now see as major injustices," reported Vox in 2020.[9] For example, her office fought to avoid releasing prisoners from California's overcrowded prisons following a US Supreme Court decision ordering the state to reduce its prison population. Harris and her supporters have defended her record, pointing to reforms such as the Back on Track program and transparency in police data.

involvement in the 2016 election. According to Harris, the investigation showed evidence that the president had obstructed justice.

A Tough Decision

Despite the buzz and support surrounding her campaign since its launch, Harris couldn't sustain fundraising or polling momentum. She lagged significantly behind other top Democratic contenders in pulling in the massive amounts of donations needed to fund a presidential campaign. By September 2019, her polling average had dropped below 10 percent as Biden, Warren, and Sanders became clearer front-runners.[10] Still, in November, Harris gave an energized speech in Iowa, repeating, "Justice is on the ballot!"[11]

At that point, Harris decided to take a close look at her campaign's future. Although she qualified for the sixth Democratic debate, she lacked the resources necessary to continue. Her campaign was widely reported to be experiencing internal turmoil and layoffs. Harris didn't see a path forward to becoming the Democratic nominee.

On December 3, 2019, Harris announced that she was suspending her campaign and withdrawing from

Though she attracted passionate support, Harris was unable to secure the polling numbers and funding to sustain her presidential campaign.

the presidential race. "I've taken stock and looked at this from every angle, and over the last few days have come to one of the hardest decisions of my life," she wrote. She vowed that she would continue in what she saw as the fight for America. "Although I am no longer running for president, I will do everything in my power to defeat Donald Trump and fight for the future of our country and the best of who we are."[12]

SUPERHEROES ARE EVERYWHERE

Harris became a children's book author in 2019. In her book *Superheroes Are Everywhere*, illustrated by Mechal Renee Roe, Harris shares how she was shaped by role models as she grew up. She explains that everyone has the power to make the world better. "I've met strong, resilient kids who I knew could have wonderful futures if they learned to believe in themselves and find good role models," she said in a promotional video for the book's release.[13]

CHAPTER
EIGHT

CALLS FOR JUSTICE

After her withdrawal from the presidential race, Harris turned her focus back to Congress. The legislative body was about to take a significant action. On December 18, 2019, the House of Representatives approved articles of impeachment against President Trump. He was impeached on two articles: abuse of power and obstruction of Congress. The impeachment stemmed from a phone call between Trump and the Ukrainian president. Democrats accused Trump of withholding military aid to Ukraine in exchange for the country investigating the business dealings of the Biden family. Trump denied doing this, and he said that his goal had been to investigate corruption in Ukraine. The following month, the articles were submitted to the Senate, resulting in an impeachment trial. Trump was the third president in US history to be impeached, following Andrew Johnson in 1868 and Bill Clinton in 1998.

Harris walks toward the Senate chamber for the impeachment trial of President Trump.

On February 5, Harris made her first statement on the Senate floor since withdrawing her presidential bid. She stated that she would be voting to convict Trump on both articles of impeachment. Harris did not believe Trump's explanation that he sought to investigate corruption, and she believed the phone call warranted his removal from office. Later that day, the Senate voted on the impeachment articles. It acquitted Trump on both counts. All senators voted along party lines, except for Republican senator Mitt Romney, who broke with his party in voting to convict Trump on abuse of power.

Meanwhile, the race for the Democratic nomination continued. The candidate pool narrowed to two people

REMEMBERING BLOODY SUNDAY

Harris recorded her endorsement video for Biden from Selma, Alabama, as she commemorated the 55th anniversary of an event known as Bloody Sunday. On March 7, 1965, 600 civil rights activists marched across the Edmund Pettus Bridge in Selma. They were making their way to Montgomery, 54 miles (87 km) away, to protest for voting rights.[1] On the bridge, protesters were confronted by state troopers and deputies, some waving Confederate flags. The police beat the protesters with clubs and other weapons, shooting tear gas at them. One protester was shot and killed. Activist John Lewis was part of the group of protesters. He became a congressman in 1987. "I thought I was going to die," he remembered in a tweet posted in March 2020. "I don't know how I made it back, but I know we cannot rest. . . . We must keep pushing and pulling and finding a way to get in the way."[2] Lewis passed away on July 17, 2020.

by the beginning of March: Biden and Sanders. On March 8, Harris posted a video to Twitter endorsing Biden for president. "I believe in Joe," she said. "We need a leader who really does care about the people and who can unify the people."[3] Biden became the presumptive nominee when Sanders dropped out in April.

A Racial Reckoning

On May 25, 2020, a Black man named George Floyd died in Minneapolis after a white police officer knelt on Floyd's neck for several minutes. This event ignited demands for justice. Large-scale protests against racism and police brutality spread throughout the country. Some protests turned into riots. Police reform and civil unrest both became major issues during the 2020 presidential campaign. In the days following Floyd's death, Harris joined with protesters calling for racial justice outside the White House in Washington, DC. "Our country can no longer accept the status quo where Black people are treated as less than human," she wrote in a *Los Angeles Sentinel* opinion piece.[4] She also voiced her support for directing funding away from police departments and toward organizations that would address deeper social issues such as poverty, education,

Following the death of George Floyd, Harris and other senators observed a moment of silence at the US Capitol on June 4, 2020.

and mental health. The idea received pushback. Opponents said shifting resources away from law enforcement would leave communities less safe.

Again, Harris was the target of skepticism and criticism from both sides of the political aisle. Conservatives said she didn't support law enforcement and was too far to the political left. Progressives pointed to her past roles as prosecutor and attorney general, saying she had supported what they saw as an unjust system that punished people too harshly.

Harris used her law enforcement background to generate ideas for police reform. A little over a week after Floyd's death, Harris joined with Congressional Black Caucus chair Karen Bass, Senator Cory Booker, and House Judiciary Committee chair Jerry Nadler to introduce the George Floyd Justice in Policing Act of 2020. In a statement, the lawmakers said the legislation was meant to "hold police accountable, change the

SAYING THEIR NAMES

On May 25, 2020, Minneapolis police officers detained a 46-year-old Black man named George Floyd on a city street. A white officer, Derek Chauvin, held Floyd on the ground with his knee pressed to Floyd's neck for about eight minutes as Floyd and onlookers begged the officer to release him. Floyd was later pronounced dead at a hospital. The incident was captured on video, and Floyd's repeated statement of "I can't breathe" became a rallying cry for thousands of outraged protesters who took to the streets in cities around the country. In some cases, the protests became violent riots in which people fought police and destroyed buildings and property.

Following the Floyd case, protesters demanded justice for others killed by police, such as Breonna Taylor, a Black woman killed earlier in the year by police in her Kentucky apartment during a botched raid. On August 23, 2020, police shot a Black man named Jacob Blake in Kenosha, Wisconsin, paralyzing him and leading to further protests against police brutality. Activists pointed to the violence as proof that structural change was needed, citing names of other Black people who had been killed by police in recent years, including Michael Brown, Eric Garner, Philando Castile, and others.

culture of law enforcement, and build trust between law enforcement and our communities."[5] Among its wide-ranging features were the prohibition of racial, religious, and discriminatory profiling as well as bans on choke holds and no-knock warrants. It also called for the creation of a national registry on police misconduct to keep officers accountable. It included requirements for law enforcement to report data, undergo implicit bias training, and wear body cameras. The bill passed in the House of Representatives, but it stalled in the Senate, where Republicans supported their own police reform bill.

Vice Presidential Pick

On August 11, 2020, Biden announced that he had selected Harris as his running mate in the race for president. Harris had been a top contender for the position and was thought to be someone who could energize the Democratic base as the long campaign neared its conclusion. High-profile supporters such as Obama, Sanders, and Hillary Clinton applauded the choice. For many people, Harris's nomination held special significance because she is a Black woman. Representative Barbara Lee of California said, "Here

Biden and Harris spoke jointly at a Wilmington, Delaware, high school the day after Biden announced he had chosen her as his running mate.

you have now this remarkable, brilliant, prepared African-American woman, South Asian woman, ready to fulfill the dreams and aspirations of Shirley Chisholm and myself and so many women of color. This is exciting and is finally a breakthrough that so many of us have been waiting for. And it didn't come easy."[6]

Republicans criticized Harris, who would now be part of the opposing presidential ticket in the November election. The chair of the Republican National Committee, Ronna McDaniel, said that Harris held "extreme positions." Even so, many who criticized her also admitted she was a force to be reckoned with. Republican senator Lindsey Graham of South Carolina called her "smart," "aggressive," and a "formidable opponent."[7]

On August 19, 2020, Harris accepted the Democratic vice presidential nomination on the third night of the Democratic National Convention. Because of the COVID-19 pandemic, the event had been postponed and downsized. Most of the presenters attended remotely from different locations across the country. Harris and Biden both spoke remotely from Delaware's Chase Center.

In her acceptance speech, Harris talked about her life, family, and career. She highlighted women of the past who paved the way. "There's another woman, whose name isn't known, whose story isn't shared," she said. "Another woman whose shoulders I stand on. And that's my mother—Shyamala Gopalan Harris."[8] She also spoke about her respect for Joe Biden and her friendship with his son, Beau. Calling out the importance of service, justice, and fair treatment, she outlined challenges facing the country, including the pandemic, systemic racism, and inequities. "Years from now, this moment will have passed," she said. "And our

Like many events in 2020, the Democratic National Convention was converted to a largely digital format, with party members and supporters watching the proceedings online.

children and our grandchildren will look in our eyes and ask us: 'Where were you when the stakes were so high?' They will ask us, 'What was it like?' And we will tell them. We will tell them, not just how we felt. We will tell them what we did."[9]

CHAPTER NINE

MAKING HISTORY AGAIN

As the 2020 presidential election approached, America was facing challenges on several fronts. In late September, the US death toll from COVID-19 passed 200,000.¹ Businesses, schools, and organizations struggled with mandated lockdowns and other restrictions resulting from the pandemic, causing layoffs and other financial stresses. The economy had taken a brutal hit. October 2 brought shocking news when President Trump announced that he and First Lady Melania Trump had tested positive for COVID-19. They soon recovered. Meanwhile, protests and unrest continued as demonstrators called for racial justice and police reforms. At every turn, the leaders of the opposing political parties seemed to be at odds, with no clear path forward.

Another hot button issue presented itself when a position on the Supreme Court opened following the

Due to the pandemic, many campaign events were held outdoors and with social distancing protocols in place.

death of Justice Ruth Bader Ginsburg in September. While Republicans wanted to fast-track their own nominee, Amy Coney Barrett, Democrats cried foul, asserting that the nomination for the next justice should take place after voters had their say in the November election. All of these issues had combined for an increasingly bitter presidential race that seemed to spotlight the country's severe divisions.

LEGACY OF RBG

Born in 1933 in Brooklyn, New York, Ruth Bader Ginsburg became a champion for women's rights. Among her accomplishments, she became the first female tenured professor at Columbia Law School and established the Women's Rights Project at the American Civil Liberties Union. Throughout the 1970s and 1980s, she led what NPR later called a "legal crusade for women's rights."[2] She was appointed to the Supreme Court in 1993 by President Bill Clinton. In her 27 years on the court, she became a feminist icon. Toward the end of her career she became known for her passionate dissenting opinions and earned the pop-culture nickname RBG. Ginsburg died on September 18, 2020, at age 87. In a tribute to Ginsburg, Harris wrote, "She never forgot where she came from, or those who sacrificed to help her grow into the historic icon we all came to revere."[3] On September 26, President Trump announced he would be nominating federal judge Amy Coney Barrett to the Supreme Court to fill Ginsburg's vacancy. A month later, the Senate confirmed Barrett's appointment by a vote of 52–48.[4]

Vice Presidential Debate

On October 7, millions of Americans tuned in to the vice presidential debate between Harris and Mike Pence, the Republican candidate running alongside Donald Trump for reelection. The first of three planned presidential debates had taken place the week before between Biden and Trump, and the event had quickly devolved into interruptions and personal attacks. The vice presidential candidates would have just one debate. Harris knew that all eyes would be on her performance, which would affect not only the upcoming election but also the future of her political career.

Although the vice presidential debate remained more civil than its presidential counterpart, it showed the starkly opposed positions of the two candidates. Harris criticized the Trump administration's handling of the pandemic and its efforts to overturn the Affordable Care Act, a health-care reform act passed under the Obama administration. Pence accused Harris of doing nothing for criminal justice reform in California and contended that she and Biden would raise taxes. Harris defended her record, saying, "I will not sit here and be lectured by the vice president on what it means to enforce the laws of our country. I am the only one on this stage who has personally prosecuted everything from child sexual assault to homicide."[5]

Harris brought up the president's previous failures to disavow white supremacists, while Pence denied that systemic racism existed. Another topic was protecting the environment. The Trump administration had withdrawn from the Paris Agreement, an international climate change treaty, and had removed environmental regulations. The Trump administration believed that such agreements and regulations unnecessarily harmed certain industries. The Biden-Harris team vowed to rejoin the agreement and put forward new plans to address climate change.

"I'M SPEAKING"

During the vice presidential debate, Harris created a buzz with a remark to Pence as he interrupted her. "Mr. Vice President, I'm speaking," she said.[6] The phrase lit up social media and was quickly reproduced in memes and on T-shirts, with many commenters calling the moment relatable. "Kamala Harris is every woman trying to be heard," announced *Vogue*.[7] It wasn't the first time that people had called attention to Harris being interrupted. In the Senate, observers had noted that she appeared to be interrupted more than her male colleagues.

A Long Election

Election Day was set for November 3. However, a record number of voters cast their

Harris and Vice President Mike Pence faced off in a contentious debate on October 7, 2020.

votes early or voted by mail, allowing them to avoid large Election Day crowds in the midst of the pandemic. As expected, large numbers of mail-in ballots delayed the projection of a clear winner in swing states. On the morning of Saturday, November 7, major news organizations named Biden and Harris as the projected winners following their electoral win in Pennsylvania, a battleground state. Harris's team posted a video on her social media channels of her speaking to Biden over the phone after their victory was declared. "We did it, Joe," she said.[8] When the vote counts were final, the Biden and Trump camps both posted record-breaking numbers of individual votes for a presidential race, with Biden-Harris earning more than 81 million and

Trump-Pence capturing more than 74 million.[9] The previous record had been the 69.5 million votes Barack Obama received in 2008.[10]

That evening, Harris walked onto the stage in Delaware to give her victory speech. "To the American people: No matter who you voted for, I will strive to be the vice president that Joe was to President Obama—loyal, honest, and prepared, waking up every day thinking of you and your families," she said.[11] She shared some of her personal history, recognizing the importance of the women who came before her and giving a tribute to her mother.

Harris and Biden's transition into the White House would come with challenges. Trump contested the results of the election and did not concede. He and his legal team looked for ways to overturn the results, and he called the election "rigged."[12] On election night, he had declared falsely that he was the winner. Leading up to the election and after, he claimed there was widespread voter fraud. This was denied by voting officials in each state. After the election, Attorney General William Barr reported that the US Justice Department had found no evidence of widespread fraud that would change the election's outcome.

In December 2020 and January 2021, Harris and Biden worked to make and announce appointments to key positions in the executive branch.

Normally, the president-elect's team would receive funds, information, and offices for its transition into power. To officially begin the transition, the head of the General Services Administration (GSA) is required to initiate the process by signing what is called a letter of ascertainment to confirm the winner of the election. However, the GSA's leader, Emily Murphy, declined to sign the letter as quickly after the election as past GSA leaders had done. The delay meant that the transition team could not receive funds allocated for the transition, access national security information, or be briefed by officials. On November 23, Murphy signed the letter to initiate the transition, stating that she believed the outcome was now certain enough to do so.

The Trump team filed legal challenges in several states, but any that would affect the outcome were dismissed by the courts. The Trump campaign requested recounts in close states, and the results of these recounts in Georgia and Wisconsin showed that Biden remained the winner. By early December, the results of each state had been certified. On Monday, December 14, the presidential electors of the electoral college formally cast their votes. Biden was the winner.

Charting a New Course

As Harris and Biden looked forward to their inauguration on January 20, 2021, their teams were ready to hit the ground running. Their slogan was "Build Back Better." Soon after their victory speeches, Biden announced a COVID-19 task force. The two set up a website for the transition and began filling positions on their teams.

Harris chose women to make up her key staff, including experienced Democratic staffer and public policy adviser Tina Flournoy as chief of staff. Others included Rohini Kosoglu as domestic policy adviser and Nancy McEldowney as national security adviser, as well as Symone Sanders and Ashley Etienne on her communications staff. The transition website highlighted four key priorities for Biden and Harris: COVID-19, economic recovery, racial equity, and climate change.

A Dramatic Inauguration

There was one more step to finalize the results of the election. On January 6, both houses of Congress met to certify the electoral college results. As vice president, Pence would preside over the certification. At the same time, Trump spoke at an event called the Save America Rally near the US Capitol. He called on his supporters to march to the Capitol and pressure Pence and members of Congress to reject electoral votes from several states to overturn Biden's victory.

As Trump's speech ended, thousands of his supporters moved toward the Capitol. Later, many pushed past police

> **THE VICE PRESIDENT'S ROLE**
>
> The US Constitution assigns the role of certifying electoral votes to the vice president. This is typically a largely ceremonial role. Members of Congress can object to electoral votes, and several did so following the 2020 election. The vice president's job is to oversee the counting. Trump and some supporters, claiming that some electors were chosen fraudulently, urged Pence to reject those votes. Pence declined to do so. In response, some of those who stormed the US Capitol on January 6 chanted "Hang Mike Pence."[13]

and barriers, smashed doors and windows, and broke into the Capitol building. Security forces evacuated lawmakers, including Harris, in the middle of the certification process, and the rioters spread through the building. A police officer shot and killed one of the rioters. One police officer died from injuries he sustained at the hands of other rioters.

By the evening, the police had secured the building, and lawmakers resumed their work. Late that night, they formally certified the victory of Biden and Harris. The next day, Harris said, "What we saw yesterday in our nation's capital was, as the President-elect has called it, an assault on the rule of law. And it has no place in our democracy."[14]

The Biden-Harris inauguration was set for January 20. The events of January 6 meant that the ceremony, already reduced in scope due to the COVID-19 pandemic, would have heightened security. Tens of thousands of National Guard troops arrived in Washington, DC, to protect the capital city. Tensions were high in Washington and around the country, but the inauguration was carried out smoothly and safely. Biden and Harris took their oaths of office shortly before noon.

Harris takes the oath of office from Supreme Court justice Sonia Sotomayor.

Kamala Harris has been a trailblazer throughout her career, from her rise through the legal system, into the world of politics, and upward to one of the highest offices in the country. From an early age growing up in California's Bay Area, Harris had carried the values of justice, pride, and hard work instilled in her by her mother and important mentors as she looked to make positive change. Now a nation looked to her for leadership and healing, and supporters and detractors alike would be watching closely. As she made history by entering the White House, a new generation of young girls could at last see someone who looked like them in the nation's halls of power.

TIMELINE

1964
Kamala Harris is born in Oakland, California, on October 20.

1981
Harris graduates from Westmount High School in Quebec.

1986
Harris graduates from Howard University in Washington, DC.

1989
Harris graduates from the University of California, Hastings College of the Law, passing the California bar exam the following year.

1990
Harris begins working at Alameda County in California as deputy district attorney.

1998
Harris begins working at the San Francisco district attorney's office.

2003
Harris is elected district attorney of San Francisco, becoming the first Black woman and first South Asian woman to be a district attorney in California.

2009
On February 11, Harris's mother, Shyamala, dies of cancer.

2010
Harris is elected attorney general of California in a close race.

TIMELINE

2014
On August 22, Harris marries Doug Emhoff and becomes stepmother to his children, Cole and Ella; Harris is reelected attorney general of California.

2016
Harris is elected to the US Senate.

2019
On January 21, Harris announces her presidential bid on *Good Morning America*; on June 27, she participates in her first Democratic Party presidential primary debate in Miami; on December 3, she announces that she is suspending her presidential campaign.

2020
February
On February 5, Harris votes in favor of convicting president Donald Trump on both counts of impeachment.
March
On March 8, Harris endorses Joe Biden for president.

2020

May
On May 25, George Floyd dies following an encounter with a Minneapolis police officer, sparking nationwide protests and leading Harris to join racial justice demonstrations and introduce police reform legislation.

August
On August 11, Biden announces Harris as his running mate; on August 19, the third night of the Democratic National Convention, she formally accepts the vice presidential nomination.

October
On October 7, Harris participates in the single vice presidential debate, facing off against Republican Mike Pence.

November
On November 3, Election Day, US citizens cast their votes for the presidential election; on November 7, major media organizations declare Harris and Biden the winners of the 2020 election, and they give their victory speeches outside the Chase Center in Wilmington, Delaware.

2021

On January 20, Harris is inaugurated as vice president of the United States.

ESSENTIAL FACTS

Date of Birth
October 20, 1964

Place of Birth
Oakland, California

Parents
Donald Harris and Shyamala Gopalan Harris

Education
Howard University; University of California, Hastings College of the Law

Marriage
Doug Emhoff (2014)

Stepchildren
Cole, Ella

Career Highlights
In 2003, Harris was elected district attorney of San Francisco. In 2010, she was elected attorney general of California. In 2016, she was elected as a US senator for California. In the Senate, Harris gained attention for her criticism of the policies of President Donald Trump. In January 2019, Harris launched a run for president but withdrew by the end of the year. The following August, Democratic presidential candidate Joe Biden announced

Harris as his running mate. They won the 2020 election, making Harris the first female vice president in US history.

Societal Contributions

Throughout her career, Harris fought to support the rights of women, people of color, immigrants, the LGBTQ community, and other groups. Harris broke many barriers, including becoming the first woman and first Black person to serve as California's attorney general. In 2020, she became the first woman, first Black person, and first Asian American elected US vice president.

Conflicts

Throughout her legal and political career, Harris has had critics from both sides of the aisle. Some disagreed with her calls to reform the justice system; others said she wasn't progressive enough. People criticized her work as attorney general, saying she participated in an unjust system, and doubted her willingness to bring about real reform. Others questioned the consistency of her positions on important issues like prison reform. While running for office, Harris experienced sexist and racist comments.

Quote

"While I may be the first woman in this office, I will not be the last." —*Kamala Harris, election victory speech, November 7, 2020*

GLOSSARY

apartheid
The historic policy of segregation in South Africa.

bipartisan
Involving cooperation between the two major political parties.

civil rights movement
The fight for racial equality in the United States in the 1950s and 1960s.

conspiracy theory
A belief, without proof, that someone is responsible for an event or crime.

desegregate
To undo the practice of separating groups of people based on race, gender, ethnicity, or other factors.

human trafficking
A form of modern-day slavery that involves the trade and purchase of human beings for exploitation in forced labor and sexual slavery.

impeach
To charge an elected official with wrongdoing.

LGBTQ
An acronym referring to lesbian, gay, bisexual, transgender, and queer or questioning people.

lynching
The act of illegally killing a person through mob action.

marginalized
Excluded or treated as unimportant or of a lower class.

pandemic
The worldwide spread of a disease.

rhetoric
Language intended to influence people, even if it may not be completely truthful.

socialist
A person in favor of a system in which the economy is controlled by communities or countries, rather than by the decisions of individuals.

sorority
A college or university social society for women.

systemic
Part of an entire system.

truancy
Staying away from school without a good excuse.

white supremacist
Someone who believes that white people are superior to all other races.

ADDITIONAL RESOURCES

Selected Bibliography

Herndon, Astead W. "Kamala Harris." *New York Times*, 22 Sept. 2020, nytimes.com. Accessed 16 Nov. 2020.

Kim, Catherine, and Zack Stanton. "55 Things You Need to Know about Kamala Harris." *Politico*, 11 Aug. 2020, politico.com. Accessed 16 Nov. 2020.

Prakash, Neha. "Read the Full Transcript of Kamala Harris's Victory Speech as Vice-President Elect," *Yahoo Finance*, yahoo.com, 7 Nov. 2020. Accessed 18 Nov. 2020.

Further Readings

Cummings, Judy Dodge. *Hillary Clinton: Groundbreaking Politician*. Abdo, 2017.

Gale, Ryan. *Joe Biden: 46th US President*. Abdo, 2021.

Harris, Kamala. *The Truths We Hold: An American Journey*. Philomel, 2019.

Online Resources

To learn more about Kamala Harris, please visit **abdobooklinks.com** or scan this QR code. These links are routinely monitored and updated to provide the most current information available.

Places to Visit
United States Capitol Building
First St. SE
Washington, DC 20004
202-226-8000
visitthecapitol.gov
The US Senate meets in the Capitol building. Visitors can tour the building and learn about its historical significance.

The White House
1600 Pennsylvania Ave. NW
Washington, DC 20500
202-456-1111
whitehouse.gov
The Vice President's Office is located in the West Wing of the White House. Visitors are able to tour the White House and learn about the history of the presidents and vice presidents who worked there.

SOURCE NOTES

Chapter 1. The First but Not the Last

1. Adam Edelman. "Clinching Victory, President-Elect Biden Declares 'Time to Heal in America.'" *NBC News*, 7 Nov. 2020, nbcnews.com. Accessed 16 Nov. 2020.

2. "Read the Full Transcript of Kamala Harris's Victory Speech." *Yahoo Finance*, 7 Nov. 2020, finance.yahoo.com. Accessed 18 Nov. 2020.

3. Kamala Harris. *The Truths We Hold*. E-book, Penguin, 2019. Location 3620.

4. Jenni Marsh et al. "November 8 Coronavirus News." *CNN*, 9 Nov. 2020, cnn.com. Accessed 16 Nov. 2020.

Chapter 2. From California to Canada

1. David Greene. "Sen. Kamala Harris Announces 2020 Presidential Candidacy." *NPR*, 21 Jan. 2019, npr.org. Accessed 6 Dec. 2020.

2. Katherine J. Igoe and Bianca Rodriguez. "Who Is Kamala Harris's Dad Donald Harris?" *Marie Claire*, 6 Nov. 2020, marieclaire.com. Accessed 11 Dec. 2020.

3. Kamala Harris. *The Truths We Hold*. E-book, Penguin, 2019. Location 211.

4. Harris, *The Truths We Hold*, Location 343.

5. Matthew Delmont. "There's a Generational Shift in the Debate over Busing." *Atlantic*, 1 July 2019, theatlantic.com. Accessed 26 Nov. 2020.

6. Harris, *The Truths We Hold*, Location 266.

7. Harris, *The Truths We Hold*, Location 395.

8. Harris, *The Truths We Hold*, Location 343.

Chapter 3. Learning the Law

1. Kamala Harris. *The Truths We Hold*. E-book, Penguin, 2019. Location 165.

2. Harris, *The Truths We Hold*, Location 169.

3. Gene Demby. "Let's Talk about Kamala Harris." *NPR*, 14 Oct. 2020, npr.org. Accessed 8 Feb. 2021.

4. Harris, *The Truths We Hold*, Location 475.

5. Harris, *The Truths We Hold*, Location 742.

6. "Three Strikes Basics." *Stanford Law School*, n.d., law.stanford.edu. Accessed 12 Dec. 2020.

Chapter 4. Against the Odds

1. David Siders. "'Ruthless': How Kamala Harris Won Her First Race," *Politico*, 24 Jan. 2019, politico.com. Accessed 12 Dec. 2020.

2. Siders, "'Ruthless.'"

3. Catherine Kim and Zack Stanton. "55 Things You Need to Know about Kamala Harris." *Politico*, 11 Aug. 2020, politico.com. Accessed 16 Nov. 2020.

4. Kyung Lah. "How Kamala Harris' Death Penalty Decisions Broke Hearts on Both Sides." *CNN*, 8 Apr. 2019, cnn.com. Accessed 21 Nov. 2020.

5. Kamala Harris. "Finding the Path Back on Track." *HuffPost*, 25 May 2011, huffpost.com. Accessed 21 Nov. 2020.

6. Jason B. Johnson. "San Francisco D.A. Creates Environmental Unit." *SFGate*, 1 June 2005, sfgate.com. Accessed 12 Dec. 2020.

7. Kim and Stanton, "55 Things You Need to Know."

8. Ed O'Keefe. "Kamala Harris: Concerns about My Prosecutorial Record Are 'Overblown.'" *CBS News*, 23 June 2019, cbsnews.com. Accessed 22 Nov. 2020.

Chapter 5. California's Attorney General

1. Bridget Bowman. "When Kamala Harris Lost on Election Night, but Won Three Weeks Later." *Roll Call*, 16 July 2019, rollcall.com. Accessed 21 Nov. 2020.

2. Bowman, "When Kamala Harris Lost on Election Night."

3. Holly Thomas. "No, Kamala Harris Is Not a 'Female Barack Obama.'" *CNN*, 23 Jan. 2019, cnn.com. Accessed 13 Dec. 2020.

4. Catherine Kim and Zack Stanton. "55 Things You Need to Know about Kamala Harris." *Politico*, 11 Aug. 2020, politico.com. Accessed 16 Nov. 2020.

5. Bowman, "When Kamala Harris Lost on Election Night."

6. Kamala Harris. *The Truths We Hold*. E-book, Penguin, 2019. Location 1236.

7. Bowman, "When Kamala Harris Lost on Election Night."

8. Alexis Jones. "Kamala Harris's Attorney General Record, Explained." *Marie Claire*, 6 Oct. 2020, marieclaire.com. Accessed 12 Dec. 2020.

9. Molly Redden. "The Human Costs of Kamala Harris' War on Truancy." *HuffPost*, 29 Mar. 2019, huffpost.com. Accessed 8 Feb. 2021.

10. "Harris Announces $241 Million Settlement with Quest Diagnostics." *Office of the California AG*, 19 May 2011, oag.ca.gov. Accessed 8 Feb. 2021.

11. Harris, *The Truths We Hold*, Location 1365.

12. Phil Willon. "$25-billion Foreclosure Settlement Was a Victory for Kamala Harris in California." *Los Angeles Times*, 16 Oct. 2016, latimes.com. Accessed 8 Feb. 2021.

13. "Harris Obtains $1.1 Billion Judgement against Predatory For-Profit School Operator." *Office of the California AG*, 23 Mar. 2016, oag.ca.gov. Accessed 8 Feb. 2021.

14. Holly Honderich. "Doug Emhoff: The First 'Second Dude' in the White House." *BBC News*, 13 Nov. 2020, bbc.com. Accessed 13 Dec. 2020.

Chapter 6. Speaking Up in the Senate

1. Kamala Harris. *The Truths We Hold*. E-book, Penguin, 2019. Location 100.

2. Phil Willon. "Newly Elected Kamala Harris Vows to Defy Trump on Immigration." *Los Angeles Times*, 10 Nov. 2016, latimes.com. Accessed 28 Nov. 2020.

3. Erica Chenoweth and Jeremy Pressman. "This Is What We Learned by Counting the Women's Marches." *Washington Post*, 7 Feb. 2017, wapo.com. Accessed 8 Feb. 2021.

4. Julie Westfall. "California Sen. Kamala Harris Strikes Defiant Tone at Women's March on Washington." *Morning Call*, 21 Jan. 2017, mcall.com. Accessed 8 Feb. 2021.

5. Jessica Estepa. "Social Media Lights Up after Kamala Harris Questions Jeff Sessions." *USA Today*, 13 June 2017, usatoday.com. Accessed 28 Nov. 2020.

6. Jack Arnholz. "When Kamala Harris Took on Brett Kavanaugh and Bill Barr." *ABC News*, 12 Aug. 2020, abcnews.go.com. Accessed 13 Dec. 2010.

SOURCE NOTES CONTINUED

7. Arnholz, "When Kamala Harris Took on Brett Kavanaugh and Bill Barr."
8. Eric Bradner, Gregory Krieg, and Caroline Kenny. "2020 Insight: Kamala Harris: 'That Is a Prison.'" *CNN*, 23 June 2018, cnn.com. Accessed 13 Dec. 2020.
9. P. R. Lockhart. "After More Than 200 Attempts, the Senate Has Finally Passed Anti-Lynching Legislation." *Vox*, 21 Dec. 2018, vox.com. Accessed 13 Dec. 2020.
10. Lockhart, "The Senate Has Finally Passed Anti-Lynching Legislation."
11. Daniella Cheslow. "Puerto Rico Releases Data on Hundreds of Deaths Following Hurricane Maria." *NPR*, 13 June 2018, npr.org. Accessed 8 Feb. 2021.
12. "Senator Harris Delivers Commencement Address at Howard University." *Kamala D. Harris, US Senate*, 13 May 2017, harris.senate.gov. Accessed 11 Dec. 2020.

Chapter 7. Running for President

1. Scott Detrow and Jessica Taylor. "Sen. Kamala Harris Announces 2020 Presidential Candidacy." *NPR*, 21 Jan. 2019, npr.org. Accessed 29 Nov. 2020.
2. Christopher Cadelago and Carla Marinucci. "Harris Kicks Off Campaign by Laying Into Trump." *Politico*, 27 Jan. 2019, politico.com. Accessed 29 Nov. 2020.
3. Sam Levin. "Kamala Harris Enters 2020 Bid with Tribute to Woman Who Broke Barriers." *Guardian*, 21 Jan. 2019, theguardian.com. Accessed 11 Dec. 2020.
4. Janet Hook and Evan Halper. "Joe Biden Pushed on the Defensive by Kamala Harris and Others." *Los Angeles Times*, 27 June 2019, latimes.com. Accessed 8 Feb. 2021.
5. Christopher Cadelago and Caitlin Oprysko. "Kamala Harris Ends Once-Promising Campaign." *Politico*, 3 Dec. 2019, politico.com. Accessed 29 Nov. 2020.
6. Juana Summers. "Kamala Harris Reports Raising $12M in 2nd Quarter." *AP News*, 5 July 2019, apnews.com. Accessed 9 Dec. 2020.
7. Scott Bixby. "Kamala Harris Built a 'Digital Army'—Now She Gets to Use It." *Daily Beast*, 12 Aug. 2020, thedailybeast.com. Accessed 6 Dec. 2020.
8. Errin Haines Whack. "AP Interview: Kamala Harris on Race and Electability in 2020." *AP News*, 8 July 2019, apnews.com. Accessed 29 Nov. 2020.
9. German Lopez. "Kamala Harris's Controversial Record on Criminal Justice, Explained." *Vox*, 12 Aug. 2020, vox.com. Accessed 19 Nov. 2020.
10. "Democratic Presidential Nomination." *RealClearPolitics*, 2020, realclearpolitics.com. Accessed 9 Dec. 2020.
11. Kamala Harris. "Justice Is on the Ballot." *Medium*, 2 Nov. 2019, kamalaharris.medium.com. Accessed 11 Dec. 2020.
12. Lissandra Villa. "Kamala Harris Dropped Out of the 2020 Presidential Race." *Time*, 3 Dec. 2019, time.com. Accessed 8 Feb. 2021.
13. "Senator Kamala Harris Shares Superheroes Are Everywhere." *YouTube*, uploaded by Penguin Kids, 9 Jan. 2019, youtube.com. Accessed 10 Dec. 2020.

Chapter 8. Calls for Justice

1. Christopher Klein. "How Selma's 'Bloody Sunday' Became a Turning Point in the Civil Rights Movement." *History*, 18 July 2020, history.com. Accessed 12 Dec. 2020.
2. Eddy Rodriguez. "Barack Obama, Cory Booker, and Others Commemorate . . . 'Bloody Sunday.'" *Newsweek*, 7 Mar. 2020, newsweek.com. Accessed 12 Dec. 2020.

3. @KamalaHarris. ".@Joe Biden has served our country with dignity." *Twitter*, 8 Mar. 2020, twitter.com. Accessed 11 Dec. 2020.

4. Kamala Harris. "A Wounded Nation: Why We Can't Give Up in the Fight for Justice." *Los Angeles Sentinel*, 3 June 2020, lasentinel.net. Accessed 9 Dec. 2020.

5. "Harris, Bass, Booker, Nadler Introduce the Justice in Policing Act of 2020." *Kamala D. Harris, US Senate*, 8 June 2020, harris.senate.gov. Accessed 9 Dec. 2020.

6. Lisa Lerer and Sydney Ember. "Kamala Harris Makes History." *New York Times*, 20 Jan. 2021, nytimes.com. Accessed 23 Feb. 2021.

7. Lauren Egan and Kristen Welker. "Trump Says Kamala Harris 'Nasty' and 'Disrespectful.'" *NBC News*, 11 Aug. 2020, nbcnews.com. Accessed 9 Dec. 2020.

8. "Harris' DNC Speech." *CNN*, 20 Aug. 2020, cnn.com. Accessed 18 Nov. 2020.

9. "Harris' DNC Speech."

Chapter 9. Making History Again

1. Emily Shapiro. "200,000 Americans Have Died from Coronavirus." *ABC News*, 22 Sept. 2020, abcnews.go.com. Accessed 8 Feb. 2021.

2. Nina Totenberg. "Justice Ruth Bader Ginsburg, Champion of Gender Equality, Dies at 87." *NPR*, 18 Sept. 2020, npr.org. Accessed 13 Dec. 2020.

3. Hilary Weaver. "'Tomorrow We Fight for Her Legacy,' Kamala Harris Says in RBG Tribute." *Elle*, 19 Sept. 2020, elle.com. Accessed 13 Dec. 2020.

4. Barbara Sprunt. "Amy Coney Barrett Confirmed to Supreme Court, Takes Constitutional Oath." *NPR*, 26 Oct. 2020, npr.org. Accessed 13 Dec. 2020.

5. Brandon Tensley. "How Kamala Harris Beat the Stereotypes during Her Historic VP Debate." *CNN*, 8 Oct. 2020, cnn.com. Accessed 12 Dec. 2020.

6. Deirdre Walsh. "4 Takeaways from the Mike Pence–Kamala Harris Vice Presidential Debate." *NPR*, 8 Oct. 2020, npr.org. Accessed 13 Dec. 2020.

7. Susan Devaney. "Kamala Harris Is Every Woman Trying to Be Heard." *Vogue*, 8 Oct. 2020, vogue.co.uk. Accessed 13 Dec. 2020.

8. @KamalaHarris. "We did it, @JoeBiden." *Twitter*, 30 July 2017, twitter.com. Accessed 11 Dec. 2020.

9. Sophie Lewis. "Joe Biden Breaks Obama's Record for the Most Votes Ever Cast." *CBS News*, 7 Dec. 2020, cbsnews.com. Accessed 13 Dec. 2020.

10. Lewis, "Joe Biden Breaks Obama's Record."

11. "Read the Full Transcript of Kamala Harris's Victory Speech as Vice-President Elect." *Yahoo Finance*, 7 Nov. 2020, finance.yahoo.com. Accessed 18 Nov. 2020.

12. @realdonaldtrump. "For years the Dems have been." *Twitter*, 13 Nov. 2020, twitter.com. Accessed 11 Dec. 2020.

13. Peter Baker et al. "Pence Reached His Limit with Trump. It Wasn't Pretty." *New York Times*, 13 Jan. 2021, nytimes.com. Accessed 8 Feb. 2021.

14. @KamalaHarris. "The challenge we're facing in our country." *Twitter*, 7 Jan. 2020, twitter.com. Accessed 11 Dec. 2020.

INDEX

Access to Counsel Act, 59
Alameda County district attorney, 8–9, 25, 27–28, 48
anti-lynching legislation, 62

Back on Track initiative, 9, 36–38, 48, 70
bar exam, 26
Barr, William, 60, 90
Barrett, Amy Coney, 86
Berkeley, California, 15, 17, 18–19, 20, 45, 52
Biden, Joe, 5, 6, 11, 12–13, 55, 57, 67–68, 71, 75, 76, 77, 80, 82, 87–94
Bloody Sunday, 76
Booker, Cory, 61, 67, 79
books, 40, 73
Braun, Carol Moseley, 56
Brown, Jerry, 35, 51, 55, 79
Bureau of Children's Justice, 9, 52
busing programs, 17–18, 67

California attorney general, 9–10, 13, 40, 43–53, 70, 78
childhood, 15–22
Chisholm, Shirley, 7, 66
Clinton, Hillary, 6, 7, 23, 55, 80
Cooley, Steve, 43, 44–45
COVID-19, 5, 11, 12, 82, 85, 87, 89, 92–93, 94
Cranston, Alan, 23

debates, 11, 67–69, 71, 87–88
Democratic National Convention, 82–83

education, 17–18, 21–23, 25–26
Emhoff, Doug, 13, 53
environmental justice, 39
Espinoza, Isaac, 34–35, 36, 44, 47

Feinstein, Dianne, 35
Ferraro, Geraldine, 6, 7
First Step Act, 63
Floyd, George, 11, 77, 79

gay/trans panic defense, 38–39
Ginsburg, Ruth Bader, 86
Good Morning America, 65
Graham, Lindsey, 82

Hallinan, Terence, 28–29, 33
Harris, Donald, 15, 16
Harris, Maya, 15, 17, 18, 20, 21, 23, 45, 53, 65
Harris, Shyamala Gopalan, 7, 8, 15–20, 34, 41, 82
Howard University, 22–23, 25, 27, 40, 63
human trafficking, 10, 31, 52–53
Hurricane Maria, 63

immigration, 10, 56–57, 58, 59, 61, 65
Immigration and Customs Enforcement, US, 59, 61
implicit bias training, 48, 80

Kavanaugh, Brett, 60–61
Kelly, John, 59
KHive, 12, 69

LGBTQ rights, 11, 38–39, 51

Marshall, Thurgood, 27, 40
McDaniel, Ronna, 81
Mueller, Robert, 60, 70

Oakland, California, 15, 25, 35, 65
Obama, Barack, 6, 44, 55, 69, 80, 87, 90

Palin, Sarah, 6
Paul, Rand, 62
Paxton, Ken, 52
Pence, Mike, 11, 87–88, 90, 93
presidential campaign, 65–73
Puerto Rico, 63

Quebec, Canada, 21

Rainbow Sign, 20
Romney, Mitt, 76

San Francisco district attorney, 9, 28, 30–31, 33–41
Sanchez, Loretta, 55
Sanders, Bernie, 67, 71, 77, 80
Scott, Tim, 61
Senate, US
  caucuses, 10
  committees, 10, 57, 60, 61
  election to, 10, 55

Sessions, Jeff, 60
Shelton, Regina, 18–19, 20, 21, 45
Simon, Lateefah, 36
Supreme Court, US, 27, 51–52, 60, 70, 85–86

three strikes law, 29–30, 39
Till, Emmett, 62
truancy, 39–40, 45–46, 47
Trump, Donald, 6, 10–11, 12, 55–61, 63, 66, 69, 70, 73, 75–76, 85, 86, 87–93
Trump, Melania, 85
2020 presidential election, 5–8, 11–12
  campaign, 80–83, 85–88
  Election Day, 12, 88–89
  inauguration, 12, 92, 94
  projection of a winner, 12, 89
  transition, 12, 90–93

Ukraine, 75
University of California, Hastings College of the Law, 25–26
US Capitol riot, 93–94

Women's March on Washington, 57–58
women's suffrage, 7

ABOUT THE AUTHOR

Laura K. Murray
Laura K. Murray is a Minnesota-based author of more than 80 books on subjects ranging from music and pop culture to history and science.

ABOUT THE CONSULTANT

Rachel Blum, PhD
Rachel Blum, PhD, is a political science professor at the University of Oklahoma in the Department of Political Science and the Carl Albert Congressional Research and Studies Center. Her research focuses on political parties in the United States, and she is the author of *How the Tea Party Captured the GOP: Insurgent Factions in American Politics*. She completed her PhD in government at Georgetown University in 2016.